CARPENTERS' HALL,

Chestnut Street, bet. 3rd and 4th,)

AND ITS

HISTORIC MEMORIES.

PUBLISHED BY THE COMPANY.

1876.

FIRST PRAYER IN CONGRESS.

CARPENTERS' HALL

AND ITS

HISTORIC MEMORIES.

The Carpenters' Company of the City and County of Philadelphia is one of the oldest Associations of Pennsylvania, being instituted about forty years after the settlement of the province by William Penn, and maintaining an uninterrupted existence from the year 1724. Among its early members were many prominent in colonial history, and whose architectural tastes are impressed upon buildings that yet remain, memorials of that early day.

The object of the Association, as expressed in its Act of Incorporation, was to obtain instruction in the science of architecture and to assist such of its members as should by accident be in need of support, and of the widows and minor children of such members.

Prominent among its founders was James Portius, who came to this country with William Penn to design and execute the proprietary building, and who, at his death in 1736, bequeathed his library of architectural works to his fellow members, thus laying the foundation of the present library of the Company. The success of the Company led to the formation of rival associations; two of these, which had inherent strength in themselves, soon saw their mistake, and negotiated for a union with their "elder brethren."

The Hall of the Company was erected in 1770, at the time Great Britain's persistent attempt "to bind the colonies in all cases whatsoever." had resulted in a general demand for a union of the colonies.

In the excitement of the period, the State House being used by the existing Government, the Hall of the Company became the great centre of gatherings for the redress of grievances or the assertion of rights, and almost all the "Town Meetings" of that eventful period were held on the lawn in front or within its walls. It began thus early to be used for civil purposes. The delegates from the "Town Meeting" in 1774 demanding the convening of the Assembly, met therein, and sent therefrom their committee to Governor Penn, whose reply was read on their return that "he saw no necessity for calling the Assembly together," on which they appointed another committee to wait upon the "Speaker of the Assembly, demanding of him a positive answer whether he would do it or not."

Among the early events in the history of Carpenters' Hall, were the memorable sessions of the "Committee of the City and County of Philadelphia" to initiate measures for calling the *first* Continental Congress—to effect which an invitation was extended to the various counties of the Province, to meet the Philadelphia Committee in conference on 15th July then next following. On FOURTH OF JULY, (by a singular coincidence) 1774, the latter appointed a sub-committee to prepare "instructions," which the then great leader of Constitutional Rights, John Dickinson thought "a duty, in order to be ready for the Provincial Committee when it should meet." This great "Provincial Committee," (so it was styled), pursuant to the call referred to, also met at Carpenters' Hall, and remained in session there till its important and effective labors were completed, July, 22d, 1774. Its Chairman was Thomas Willing, and its Clerk, Charles Thomson, and names of members as follows:

John Dickinson, Peter Chevalier, Edward Pennington, Thomas Wharton, John Cox, Joseph Reed, Thomas Wharton, Jr., Samuel Erwin, Thomas Fitzsimons, Dr. William Smith, Isaac Howell, Adam Hubley, George Schlosser, Samuel Miles, Thomas Mifflin, Christopher Ludwick, Joseph Moulder, Anthony Morris, Jr., George Gray, John Nixon, Jacob Barge, Thomas Penrose, John M. Nesbit, Jonathan B. Smith, James Mease, Thomas Barclay, Benjamin Marshall, Samuel Howell, William Moulder, John Roberts, John Bayard, William Rush.

Bucks—John Kidd, Henry Wynkoop, Joseph Kirkbride, John Wilkinson, James Wallace.

Chester—Fran. Richardson, Elisha Price, John Hart, Anthony Wayne, Hugh Lloyd, John Sellers, Francis Johnson, Richard Reiley.

Lancaster—George Ross, James Webb, Joseph Ferree, Matthias Slough, Emmanuel Carpenter, William Atlee, Alexander Lowrey, Moses Erwin.

York—James Smith, Joseph Donaldson, Thomas Hartley.

Cumberland—James Wilson, Robert Magaw, William Ervine.

Berks—Edward Biddle, Daniel Brodhead, Jonathan Potts, Thomas Dundas, Christopher Schultz.

Northampton—William Edmunds, Peter Keichlein, John Okeley, Jacob Arndt.

Northumberland—William Scull, Samuel Hunter.

Bedford—George Woods.

Westmoreland—Robert Hannah, James Carett.

This list is given, since it is rarely to be met with, and includes the names of those men who formed the *second* link (the Non-Importation Resolutions of 1765 of the merchants of Philadelphia being the *first*) in the local efforts to assert Constitutional rights. This Committee, "in a body, waited upon the Assembly then sitting" at the State House, and presented the "Instructions" to appoint delegates to represent Pennsylvania in the intended Congress, and to require them, for and on behalf of the citizens of this Province "strenuously to exert themselves to obtain a renunciation on the part of Great Britain of all powers of internal legislation for America, or of imposing taxes, &c., &c., and a repeal of every other statute particularly affecting the Province of Massachusetts Bay, passed in the last session of Parliament.

These "Instructions," with the argumentative part upon which they were predicated, were esteemed so admirable as to elicit a formal vote of thanks to their author, Mr. Dickinson, rendered (by resolution) publicly from the chair, "for the application of his eminent abilities to the service of his country."

The Assembly, by vote the day following, complied with these instructions, and appointed delegates to the "First American Congress," Amongst the members were Peyton Randolph, Samuel and John Adams, Roger Sherman, Patrick Henry, Richard Henry Lee, Christopher Gadsden, the Rutledges, and our own John Dickinson, without whom the Congress was considered incomplete, and who hence was added by the Assembly within six weeks. George Washington, too, was a member of this Congress.

They assembled at the "Merchants' Coffee House," on Second Street, near Walnut, and walked in a body to "Carpenters' Hall," the scene of their deliberations. These devoted patriots conscious of the impending perils of the movement, resolved that all their transactions, except such as they should resolve to publish, should be kept inviolably secret.

Thus, in "The Carpenters' Hall" commenced that series of deliberations which ultimated, on the 4th of July, 1776, in declaring the Colonies "Free and Independent."

BEAUTIFUL REMINISENCE OF THE FIRST AMERICAN CONGRESS, FROM THE PEN OF THE VENERABLE JOHN ADAMS,

"When the Congress met, Mr. Cushing made a motion that it should be opened with prayer. It was opposed by Mr. Jay of New York, and Mr. Rutledge of South Carolina, because we were so divided in religious sentiments—some Episcopalians, some Quakers, some Anabaptists, some Presbyterians, and some Congregationalists,—that we could not join in the same kind of worship.

Mr. Samuel Adams arose and said "that he was no bigot, and could hear a prayer from any gentleman of piety and virtue, who was at the same time a friend to his country; he was a stranger in Philadelphia, but had heard that Mr. Duché, (Duchay they pronounce it), deserved that character, and therefore he moved that Mr. Duché, an Episcopalian Clergyman might be desired to read prayers to Congress to-morrow morning." The motion was seconded and passed in the affirmative.

Mr. Randolph, our President waited upon Mr. Duché, and received for answer, that if his health would permit, he certainly would. Accordingly next morning he appeared with his clerk and in his pontificials, and read several

prayers in the established form, and then read the psalter for the 7th day of September, which was the 35th psalm—you must remember that this was the next morning after we had heard of the horrible cannonade of Boston. It seemed as if heaven had ordained that psalm to be read on that morning.

After this, Mr. Duché, unexpectedly to everybody struck out into extempore prayer, which filled the bosom of every man present—I must confess I never heard a better prayer or one so well pronounced—Episcopalian as he is, Dr. Cooper himself never prayed with such fervor, such ardor, such correctness and pathos, and in language so elegant and sublime, for America, for Congress, for the province of Massachusetts Bay, especially the town of Boston—It had excellent effect upon everybody here. I must beg you to read the psalm. If there is any faith in the Sortes Virgilianæ, or Homericæ, or especially the Sortes Biblicæ it would have been thought providential.

Here was a scene worthy of the painter's art. It was in Carpenters' Hall, in Philadelphia, a building which still survives, that the devoted individuals met to whom this service was read. Washington was kneeling there, and Henry, and Randolph, and Rutledge, and Lee, and Jay, and by their side their stood, bowed in reverence, the Puritan Patriots of New England, who at that moment had reason to believe that an armed soldiery was wasting their humble households. It was believed that Boston had been bombarded and destroyed. They prayed fervently for America, for the Congress, for the province of Massachusetts Bay and especially for the town of Boston, and who can realize the emotions with which they turned imploringly to heaven for divine interposition and aid.? It was enough, said Mr. Adams, "to melt a heart of stone." I saw the tears, gush into the eyes of the old grave pacific Quakers of Philadelphia.

One of the memorable resolves of that Congress was an address to the people of Great Britian, adopted October 21st, 1774, in which they say, "But if you are determined that your ministers shall wantonly sport with the rights of mankind—if neither the voice of Justice, the dictates of the law, the principles of the Constitution, or the suggestions of humanity, can restrain your hands from shedding human blood in such an impious cause, we must then tell you, that we will never submit to be hewers of wood or drawers of water for any ministry or nation in the world."

In an address to the inhabitants of the Colonies of the same date they say, "But we think ourselves bound in duty to observe to you, that the chemes agitated against these Colonies have been so conducted as to render it prudent that you should extend your views to mournful events, and be, in all respects, prepared for any contingency. Above all things, we earnestly entreat you, with devotion of spirit, penitence of heart, and amendment of life, to humble yourselves and implore the favor of Almighty God; and we fervently beseech his Divine goodness to take you into his gracious protection."

In Carpenters' Hall, also, met on 18th of June, 1776, a convention which exercised a controlling influence on the question of *Independence*.

The Assembly of Pennsylvania had appointed their delegates under the following "instructions."

"We strictly enjoin you, that you, on behalf of this Colony, desist from and utterly reject, any proposition, should such be made, that may cause, or lead to a separation from our Mother Country or a change in the form of government." Hence the delegates of Pennsylvania did not give their votes in Congress "for establishing government throughout the continent on the authority of the people," which Congress had recommended on the 15th of May, preceding. Richard Henry Lee had on the 7th of June, formally introduced his celebrated resolution for a *separation*, and the Pennsylvania delegates in Congress were under instructions to oppose it, when this "Provincial Conference" met. It was composed of representatives from all the counties of the Province, and was presided over by Thomas McKean; it had as members, Benjamin Franklin, Benjamin Rush, Jona. B. Smith, Henry Wynkoop, James Smith, Alexander Lowry, Joseph Heister, John Creigh, and some ninety others.

This Provincial Conference resolved that the present government of the Province was not competent for the exigencies of our affairs.

Resolved, That the present House of Assembly was not elected for the purpose of forming a new government.

Resolved, That the present House of Assembly, not having the authority of the people for that purpose, cannot proceed without assuming arbitrary powers.

Resolved, That a Provincial Convention be called for the express purpose of forming a government in the Province, on the authority of the people only.

Resolved, That we will support the measures now adopted at all hazards, be the consequences what they may.

Besides complying with the purposes for which they had been assembled, they patriotically determined to act for their constituents.

On Sunday, the 23d of June, 1776, a Committee consisting of Dr. Benjamin Rush, Col. Joseph Small, and Col. Thomas McKean, were appointed to draft a resolution declaring the sense of the Conference with respect to the independence of the Province from the crown of Great Britian, and to report next morning.

On Monday morning, the 24th of June, the Committee brought in a draft of a Declaration of Independence for the Colony of Pennsylvania, which was read by special order, and being fully considered was unanimously agreed to, in the following words:

"Whereas, George the III, King of Great Britian, &c., &c., in violation of the principles of the British Constitution, and of the laws of justice and humanity, hath, by an accumulation of oppressions unparallelled in history, excluded the inhabitants of this, with the other Colonies, from his protection.

And whereas, He hath no regard to our numerous and dutiful petitions for a redress of our complicated grievances, but hath lately purchased foreign troops to assist in enslaving us, and hath excited the savages of this country to carry on a war against us, and also the negroes to imbue their hands in the blood of their masters in a manner unpractised by civilized nations, and hath lately insulted our calamities by declaring that he will show us no mercy until he hath reduced us.

And whereas, The obligation of allegiance, being reciprocal between a king and his subjects, are now dissolved, on the side of the Colonists, by the despotism of the said king, in as much that it now appears that loyalty to him is treason against the people of this country.

And whereas, Not only the Parliament, but there is reason to believe many of the people of Great Britian have connived at the aforesaid arbitrary and unjust proceedings against us.

And whereas, The public virtue of the Colony so essential to its liberty and happiness, must be endangered by a future political union with or dependence upon a crown and nation so lost to justice, patriotism, and magnanimity. We, the deputies of the people of Pennsylvania, assembled in full Provincial Conference for forming a plan for executing the resolve of Congress of the 15th of May last, for suppressing all authority in this province derived from the crown of Great Britain, and for establishing a government on the authority of the people only, now, in this public manner, in behalf of ourselves, and with the approbation, consent, and authority of our constituents, unanimously declare our willingness to concur in a vote of Congress declaring the United Colonies Free and Independent States, provided the forming the government and the regulation of the internal affairs of this Colony be always reserved to the people of this Colony; and we do further call upon the nations of Europe, and appeal to the Great Arbiter and governor of the empires of this world, to witness for us, that this Declaration Act does not originate in ambition or in an impatience of lawful authority, but that we were driven to it in obedience to the first principles of nature, by the oppressions and cruelties of the aforesaid king and Parliament of Great Britian, as the only possible measure that was left us to preserve and establish our liberties and to transmit them inviolate to our posterity."

It was signed by eighty-five deputies, and delivered by their President to Congress. They also patriotically deter mined to act for their constituents, and to instruct the Pennsylvania delegates in Congress to concur in declaring the United Colonies Free and Independent States, and to disregard "instructions" from the Assembly, which resolution they also formerly transmitted to Congress. In prompt response to the call of this Conference, assembled the "Convention of 1776" to frame a Constitution for the Independent State of Pennsylvania. Congress adopted the Declaration of Independence on the 4th of July, and on the 15th of the same month this Convention in Carpenters' Hall ratified the action of Congress and adopted a Constitution which served as the fundamental law until the adoption of the Constitution of the United States.

In an address to his fellow citizens on the action of this "Convention" the Chairman, Thomas McKean, said, "It is now in your power to immortalize your names by mingling your achievements with the events of the year 1776—a year which we hope will be famed in the annals of history to the end of time, for establishing upon a lasting foundation the liberation of one quarter of the globe." Thus was prefigured our great Magna Charta in Carpenters' Hall, the scene of their anxious deliberations.

The use of Carpenters' Hall for the popular cause was almost continuous, and when the next Congress convened at the State House, the Committees of that body and their most important "Committee of Safety" held in their secret services within its walls. That Congress, though meeting in the State House, assembled in Carpenters' Hall to proceed in a body to the funeral of their deceased President, Peyton Randolph, October, 1775.

Christopher Marshall, in his diary, under date of October 24th, 1775, says: "Past two, went and met part of Committee at Coffee House, and from thence went in a body to Carpenters' Hall, in order to attend the funeral of Peyton Randolph (the first President of the first Continental Congress), who had departed this life suddenly after dinner, last first day, at the country house of Richard Hill: then proceeded to Christ Church, where a sermon was preached by Jacob Duché; then to Christ Church burial ground.

Among those whose manhood early appeared in a protest against the Church and State government of the early New England colonies were the Baptists. Holding among themselves all that was great in Puritanism, a manly endurance of persecution, they submitted to imprisonment and death.

Mr. Bachius was the moderator of the Warren Baptist Association of Massachusetts, and when the opposition of Great Britian stirred up a manly advocacy of liberty in the land, and in 1774 a Congress of Delegates from the Provinces met in Philadelphia, he and the suffering churches he represented thought it a proper opportunity to appeal for relief from their affliction. He therefore came to Philadelphia some time in the early fall of 1774. The Philadelphia Baptist Association was at the time in session, and he laid before them a statement of the grievances and sufferings of the New England Baptists.

A Committee was appointed to act with him in preparing a memorial to lay before Congress, and the support and assistance of all the sects not dominant in the Provinces solicited. To this responded particularly the Quakers, who, although controlling Pennsylvania, were especially obnoxious to the New Englanders. A conference between them and the Baptist Committee was held at the office of Robert Strettle Jones, a distinguished lawyer of the day.

It was finally concluded that before addressing a memorial to Congress a meeting with the delegates from New England should be had, and upon this resulted a session

IN CARPENTERS' HALL

on the 14th of October, 1774, a day worthy of commemoration.

All friends of religious liberty, in or out of Congress, were invited. John Adams, surly and indignant, Samuel Adams, Thomas Cushing, and Robert Treat Paine appeared for Massachusetts. The Catholics of Maryland were represented by Charles Carroll, of Carrolton, and his colleagues. Even Cavalier and Episcopal Virginia, appeared.

From New Jersey, James Krintzle; from Rhode Island, Stephen Hopkins and Samuel Ward; from Pennsylvania, Joseph Galloway and Thomas Mifflin, represented the sympathies of their constituents with the motives of the conference. The Quakers were particularly strong in the representation of Israel and James Pemberton and John Fox, while the Baptists stood forth with the proud representation of President Manning, of Brown University, Robert Strettle Jones, and Mr. Samuel Davis.

John Adams, in his diary, discourses with the earnestness of the Puritan and the Federalist concerning this conference. The principal speaker appears to have been Israel Pemberton, the Quaker, who, noting the grievances of his sect and others in Massachusetts Bay, John Adams accuses of Jesuitism. Says Adams; "I responded to him with great heat, not willing to hear my people thus attacked," and he declared that in Massachusetts was and ever had been the purest political liberty known.

"Then" says a record of the period, "up rose Israel Pemberton; 'John, John' he said, 'dost thou not know of the time when Friends were hung in thy colony, when Baptists were hung and whipped, and finally when Edward Shippen, a great merchant of Boston was publically whipped because he would not subscribe to the belief of thee and thy fathers, and was driven to the colony of which he afterwards became Governor?"

The conference ended at the time in nothing. But the struggle for religious liberty thus begun in Carpenters' Hall was not abandoned. Never forgotten and urged by the Catholics of Maryland, the Friends of Pennsylvania, and the Baptists of Rhode Island and New England, the cause grew until its principles were embodied in the Federal Constitution, and to-day exists in the Constitution of every State in the Union except New Hampshire.

When the British took possession, in 1777, of the city of Philadelphia, a portion of their army was quartered in the Hall, and continued there during the time they occupied the city. The soldiers made a target of the vane on the cupalo, and several holes were drilled through it by their bullets.

The early movement for the encouragement of American industries is identified with Carpenters' Hall. A public meeting of citizens was held at the Hall, and subscriptions made for that object. The following is from the papers of that day:

"The subscribers towards a fund for establishing and carrying on American manufacture of linens, woolens, &c., are requested to meet at Carpenters' Hall, on 5th day next, the 16th inst., at 3 o'clock in the afternoon, to consider a plan for carrying the same into execution." They organized; the Chairman on taking his seat said, "Poverty, with all its other evils, has joined with it in every part of Europe all the miseries of slavery. America is now the only asylum for liberty in the whole world. By establishing manufactories we stretch forth a hand from the ark and invite the timid manufacturer to come in. By bringing manufacturers into this land of liberty and plenty, we remove them from the state in which they existed in their own country, and place them in circumstances to enable them to become husbands and fathers, and add to the general tide of human happiness. In closing the imports from Great Britain, the wisdom of Congress cannot be too much admired. A people who are entirely dependent on foreigners for food and clothing must always be subject to them. That poverty, confinement, and death are trifling evils compared with that total depravity of heart which is connected with slavery. By becoming slaves we shall lose every principle of virtue; we shall transfer an unlimited obedience from our Maker to a corrupt majority of the British House of Commons, and shall esteem their crimes the certificate of their divine right to govern us. We shall cease to look upon the Court and Ministry—harpies who hover around the liberties of our country—with detestation; we shall hug our chains and cease to be men."

In 1787 the United States Commissary-General of Military Stores occupied the Hall, and from 1773 to 1790 the books of the Philadelphia Library, then the nucleus only of the magnificent collection which now exists, were also deposited there.

In 1787 sundry deputies of the convention to frame a Constitution for the United States appeared at the State House, but a majority not being present, adjourned from day to day. A quorum having arrived, they held their sessions for that time in "The Carpenters' Hall" where "they deliberated with closed doors, and at the end of four months agreed upon a Constitution for the United States of America," making the Carpenters' Hall memorial both for the first united effort to obtain a redress of grievances from the Mother Country, and the place where the Fathers of the Republic changed by the Constitution a loose league of separate States into a powerful nation.

The Hall has also been largely used for public purposes. During the Revolution it was partly used by the Commissary-General of Military Stores, and a temporary building erected by him for a "brass foundry and file cutting shop;" and at times by the Barrack Master.

In 1791 the first Bank of the United States transacted its banking business there for upwards of six years, and upon their removal to their new banking house, The "Bank of the State of Pennsylvania" occupied it until they erected their banking-house on Second street.

The United States occupied it for their Land Office for a short period, when the business of the Custom House was removed to it, and it continued as such about fourteen years, until the incorporation of the second Bank of the United States, when the United States surrendered it by agreement to that institution, which occupied it about four years.

On the removal of the Bank, the Apprentices' Library had their collection on the second story for about seven years, after which the Franklin Institute occupied the Hall and held within it the first exhibition of domestic manufactures ever offered to the American public.

The Convention for a monument to the signers of the Declaration of Independence met and held their deliberations in it.

In 1857 the Carpenters' Company, with a reverence for their old Hall which has so well stood the test of time, being connected with so many stirring incidents in our national history, in a belief that its story is instructive and valuable, withdrew it from the purpose of trade and commerce, and devoted it to their own use and the recollections of the historic memories that cluster around it, as the Nation's Birth Place.

www.ingramcontent.com/pod-product-compliance
Lightning Source LLC
LaVergne TN
LVHW020635110826
845149LV00004B/1194
* 9 7 8 1 4 1 8 1 9 0 9 2 7 *